HENRY FORD
Pioneer of Modern Industry

Greg Roza

REAL LIFE readers™

Rosen Classroom™

New York

Published in 2009 by The Rosen Publishing Group, Inc.
29 East 21st Street, New York, NY 10010

Book Design: Haley WIlson

Photo Credits: Cover © Library of Congress/Hulton Archive/Getty Images; cover (background) ©
Maugli/Shutterstock; p. 5 © Petrified Collection/Getty Images; pp. 6, 7 © Hulton Archive/Getty Images;
p. 9 © Time Life Pictures/Stringer/Getty Images; pp. 10, 18, 19 © Hulton Archive/Stringer/Getty Images;
p. 13 © MPI/Stringer/Hulton Archive/Getty Images; p. 14 © AFP/Stringer/Getty Images; p. 17 © Hulton
Collection/Hulton Archive/Getty Images; p. 21 © Ralph Morse/Stringer/Time & Life Pictures/Getty images.

ISBN: 978-1-4358-0137-0
6-pack ISBN: 978-1-4358-0138-7

Manufactured in the United States of America

CPSIA Compliance Information: Batch #WR112190RC:
For Further Information contact Rosen Publishing, New York, New York at 1-800-237-9932

Contents

Industry in America

Industry is the ordered creation of goods and services, often for a large group of people. The Industrial **Revolution**—which began in the late 1700s—was a period of great improvements in science, farming, travel, **communication**, and manufacturing.

The Industrial Revolution ended in the mid-1800s, but scientists and inventors continued to improve on the discoveries of those who had come before them. American industrial **pioneer** Henry Ford used inventions others had created—such as the **internal combustion engine** and the **assembly line**—to change the world. Ford's improvements to the manufacturing industry helped make the United States a leading world power in the twentieth century.

Some Important Inventions of the Industrial Revolution

year	invention	inventor	industry
1775	first workable steam engine	James Watt	travel, farming, manufacturing
1793	cotton gin	Eli Whitney	farming, manufacturing
1807	commercially successful steamboat	Robert Fulton	travel
1844	sewing machine	Elias Howe	clothing manufacturing
1876	telephone	Alexander Graham Bell	communication
1903	first controllable airplane	Wilbur and Orville Wright	travel

Factories, like the one shown here, drew Americans from the farms to the cities, where jobs were more plentiful.

Henry Ford's Early Years

Henry Ford was born on July 30, 1863, in the area of Michigan that's today the city of Dearborn. He was the oldest of six children. The Fords owned a successful farm, and Henry spent much of his childhood going to a one-room schoolhouse, doing chores, and learning about farm machinery.

Ford, shown here as a boy, grew up in the house shown on page 7. He had the house fixed up in 1919. In 1944, it was moved to Greenfield Village, an 80-acre museum of the Industrial Revolution located in Dearborn, Michigan.

Henry didn't like farmwork very much, but he took an interest in machines. When he was about 13, his father gave him a watch. He taught himself to take it apart and put it back together! Soon he became so good at it that friends and neighbors brought him broken watches to fix.

In 1879, Henry traveled to the nearby city of Detroit, Michigan, where he became an **apprentice** machinist. For the first time, Henry had the chance to work with steam engines and internal combustion engines on a regular basis. He learned quickly and soon got a job fixing steam engines for the Westinghouse Electric Corporation, which was a large and powerful manufacturer of electrical machinery.

Three years after leaving the family farm, Henry returned to help his father fix farm machines and do other work. He also continued to work part-time as a machinist in Detroit.

This photograph was taken in 1893, when Ford was 30 years old.

This is a photograph of the Edison Illuminating Company's employees in 1892. Ford is in the back row, third from the right.

In 1888, Ford married a local woman named Clara Bryant and moved off the family farm. He supported Clara and himself by opening a sawmill. Although he was very busy, Ford continued to work with engines. In 1891, he got a job as an **engineer** with the Edison Illuminating Company in Detroit. He became chief engineer in 1893. That same year, Clara gave birth to a boy named Edsel Bryant Ford.

Ford's new position gave him more time and money to work with internal combustion engines in his workshop. He was hard at work on an idea that would change the world.

Here Comes the Quadricycle

In his workshop, Ford constructed an automobile that used an internal combustion engine. Gasoline gave power to the engine. The engine moved a chain, which in turn moved a set of wheels. The car had two speeds, but it couldn't go backwards. The 3-gallon (11.3-l) gas tank was under the seat. Ford drove the car for the first time on June 4, 1896. It reached a top speed of 20 miles (32 km) per hour.

Ford called his invention the Quadricycle—which means "four wheels"—because it rode on four bicycle tires. Ford's boss, inventor and businessman Thomas Edison, encouraged him to keep working on his automobile.

The Quadricycle wasn't the first car ever made, but it helped spark a modern industrial revolution.
Today, Ford's original Quadricycle is on display at the Henry Ford Museum in Dearborn, Michigan.

In this 1905 photo, Ford and his son Edsel sit in a
Model F Ford automobile in front of their house in Detroit, Michigan.

After Ford had successfully tested his invention, he began planning the **mass production** of Quadricycles. He finished building a new model of the Quadricycle in 1898 and helped found the Detroit Automobile Company in 1899. This company didn't last and closed its doors in January 1901.

Ford continued to make more powerful cars. After another attempt at opening a car factory didn't work out for him, Ford finally met with success when he opened the Ford Motor Company in 1903. Thanks to well-made cars and successful marketing, the Ford automobile was soon a popular product around the country.

The Assembly Line

Soon, Ford had a lot of **competition** in the car business. He worked hard to improve his product as well as the manufacturing process. Each car was made by a team of men. It took about 12 hours to put one car together.

Ford began using the assembly line to manufacture cars in 1913. On an assembly line, the cars are moved past workers. Each worker carries out the same job on each car. Using this method, it took only about an hour and a half to make a single car! When other manufacturers saw how effective Ford's assembly lines were, they began to use them in their factories, too.

Ford came up with other ways to improve the manufacturing process. In 1914, Ford offered his workers $5.00 a day—more than twice the amount most workers received. Many talented machinists came to work for Ford, and the quality of the cars showed it.

The Great Success of the Model T

Although he made many contributions to industry and manufacturing, Ford is perhaps best remembered for the Model T. Before 1908, the Ford Motor Company had produced several models of automobiles, but Ford wanted to improve his product. He wanted to build a car that was affordable and easy to drive. He wanted it to be big enough for a family, but small enough for a single person to care for. The result was the Model T.

The Model T set records for car sales.
The 10 millionth Model T produced is shown on page 18.
The 15 millionth is shown below.

The Ford Motor Company began selling the Model T in 1908. Today it's widely recognized as America's first popular, affordable car. By 1918, more than half the cars on U.S. roads were Model Ts! The last one rolled off the assembly line in 1927.

A King of Industry

The Ford Motor Company was a great success during Ford's life. It continued to grow even after Ford passed away on April 7, 1947, at the age of 83. By this time, Ford was worth a little over $1 **billion**! This made him one of the richest people in the world.

Henry Ford didn't invent the automobile or the assembly line. However, he's remembered as the man who used the assembly line to produce cars that were affordable for all Americans. His mastery of the assembly line and the automobile helped change industrial practices around the world forever.

With the flag at half-staff, the Ford plant is deserted for Henry Ford's funeral.

Henry Ford: A Timeline

July 30, 1863 — Henry Ford is born.

1879 — Becomes an apprentice machinist.

1888 — Marries Clara Bryant.

1891 — Becomes an engineer with Edison Illuminating Company.

1893 — Becomes chief engineer of Edison Illuminating Company.

November 6, 1893 — Edsel Bryant Ford is born.

1896 — Finishes the Quadricycle.

1898 — Finishes an improved Quadricycle.

1899 — Helps found the Detroit Automobile Company.

1901 — The Detroit Automobile Company closes.

1903 — Founds the Ford Motor Company.

1908 — First Model T is made.

1913 — Ford begins using the assembly line in his factories.

1914 — Begins paying his employees $5.00 a day.

1927 — Ford Motor Company stops making the Model T.

April 7, 1947 — Ford passes away at the age of 83.

Glossary

apprentice (uh-PREHN-tihs) A person who learns a trade by working for someone who is already trained.

assembly line (uh-SEHM-blee LYN) A series of workstations at which steps in the making of a product are carried out.

billion (BIHL-yuhn) One thousand millions, or 1,000,000,000.

communication (kuh-myoo-nuh-KAY-shun) The passing back and forth of information.

competition (kahm-puh-TIH-shun) Others in the same business.

engineer (ehn-juh-NEER) A master at planning and building things, such as engines, machines, roads, or bridges.

internal combustion engine (ihn-TUHR-nuhl kuhm-BUHS-chun EHN-juhn) An engine that makes power by burning a fuel such as gasoline.

mass production (MAAS pruh-DUHK-shun) A method of making things in large amounts.

pioneer (py-uh-NEER) Someone who starts or helps to spread new ideas or things.

revolution (reh-vuh-LOO-shun) A complete change in the way things are done.

Index

A
airplane, 5
apprentice machinist, 8, 22
assembly line(s), 4, 16, 19, 20, 22

B
Bell, Alexander Graham, 5
Bryant, Clara, 11, 22

C
cotton gin, 5

D
Dearborn, Michigan, 6
Detroit Automobile Company, 15, 22
Detroit, Michigan, 8, 11

E
Edison Illuminating Company, 11, 22
Edison, Thomas, 12
engineer, 11, 22

F
farm(work), 6, 7, 8, 11
Ford, Edsel Bryant, 11, 22
Ford Motor Company, 15, 18, 19, 20, 22
Fulton, Robert, 5

H
Howe, Elias, 5

I
Industrial Revolution, 4, 5
internal combustion engine(s), 4, 8, 11, 12

M
mass production, 15
Model T(s), 18, 19, 22

Q
Quadricycle(s), 12, 15, 22

S
sawmill, 11
sewing machine, 5
steamboat, 5
steam engine(s), 5, 8

T
telephone, 5

W
Watt, James, 5
Westinghouse Electric Corporation, 8
Whitney, Eli, 5
Wright, Wilbur and Orville, 5

Due to the changing nature of Internet links, The Rosen Publishing Group, Inc., has developed an online list of Web sites related to the subject of this book. This site is updated regularly. Please use this link to access the list: http://www.rcbmlinks.com/rlr/hford